ZACHARY TAYLOR

The Presidents of the United States

George Washington
1789–1797

John Adams
1797–1801

Thomas Jefferson
1801–1809

James Madison
1809–1817

James Monroe
1817–1825

John Quincy Adams
1825–1829

Andrew Jackson
1829–1837

Martin Van Buren
1837–1841

William Henry Harrison
1841

John Tyler
1841–1845

James Polk
1845–1849

Zachary Taylor
1849–1850

Millard Fillmore
1850–1853

Franklin Pierce
1853–1857

James Buchanan
1857–1861

Abraham Lincoln
1861–1865

Andrew Johnson
1865–1869

Ulysses S. Grant
1869–1877

Rutherford B. Hayes
1877–1881

James Garfield
1881

Chester Arthur
1881–1885

Grover Cleveland
1885–1889

Benjamin Harrison
1889–1893

Grover Cleveland
1893–1897

William McKinley
1897–1901

Theodore Roosevelt
1901–1909

William H. Taft
1909–1913

Woodrow Wilson
1913–1921

Warren Harding
1921–1923

Calvin Coolidge
1923–1929

Herbert Hoover
1929–1933

Franklin D. Roosevelt
1933–1945

Harry Truman
1945–1953

Dwight Eisenhower
1953–1961

John F. Kennedy
1961–1963

Lyndon B. Johnson
1963–1969

Richard Nixon
1969–1974

Gerald Ford
1974–1977

Jimmy Carter
1977–1981

Ronald Reagan
1981–1989

George H. W. Bush
1989–1993

William J. Clinton
1993–2001

George W. Bush
2001–2009

Barack Obama
2009–

ZACHARY TAYLOR

STEVEN OTFINOSKI

mc **Marshall Cavendish**
Benchmark
New York

Published by Marshall Cavendish Benchmark
An imprint of Marshall Cavendish Corporation

Website: www.marshallcavendish.us

Other Marshall Cavendish Offices:
Marshall Cavendish International (Asia) Private Limited, 1 New Industrial Road, Singapore 536196 • Marshall Cavendish International (Thailand) Co Ltd. 253 Asoke, 12th Flr, Sukhumvit 21 Road, Klongtoey Nua, Wattana, Bangkok 10110, Thailand • Marshall Cavendish (Malaysia) Sdn Bhd, Times Subang, Lot 46, Subang Hi-Tech Industrial Park, Batu Tiga, 40000 Shah Alam, Selangor Darul Ehsan, Malaysia

Marshall Cavendish is a trademark of Times Publishing Limited

Library of Congress Cataloging-in-Publication Data

Otfinoski, Steven.
Zachary Taylor / Steven Otfinoski
p. cm. — (Presidents and their times)
Summary: "Provides comprehensive information on President Zachary Taylor and places him within his historical and cultural context. Also explored are the formative events of his times and how he responded"—Provided by publisher.
Includes bibliographical references and index.
ISBN 978-1-60870-187-2 (print)   ISBN 978-0-60870-729-4 (ebook)
1. Taylor, Zachary, 1784–1850—Juvenile literature. 2. Presidents—United States—Biography—Juvenile literature. I. Title.
E422.O85 2012
973.6 '3092—dc22
[B]
2010033363

Editor: Christine Florie
Publisher: Michelle Bisson
Art Director: Anahid Hamparian
Series Designer: Alex Ferrari

Photo research by Marybeth Kavanagh

Cover photo by dbimages/Alamy

The photographs in this book are used by permission and through the courtesy of: *The White House Historical Association* (White House Collection): 3, 79, 81R; *The Bridgeman Art Library*: Chicago History Museum, USA, 6; Delaware Art Museum, Wilmington, USA/Louisa DuPont Copeland Memorial Fund, 14; Private Collection/Peter Newark American Pictures, 18, 80L; *Alamy*: Mary Evans Picture Library, 8; North Wind Picture Archives, 21, 61; Pictorial Press Ltd, 48; *North Wind Picture Archives*: 10, 11, 29, 55; *The Granger Collection, NYC*: 13, 25, 50, 65; *Getty Images*: Hulton Archive, 16, 46; MPI, 22, 32, 35, 37, 40, 72; Stock Montage, 23; National Archive/Newsmakers, 43, 81L; *SuperStock*: Visual & Written, 28, 58; *Library of Congress*: 34, 80R; *Everett Collection*: 39, 70, 74; *Newscom*: Picture History, 45, 53, 69, 75; *The Image Works*: Mary Evans Picture Library, 51

Printed in Malaysia
1 3 5 6 4 2

CONTENTS

★ ★ ★ ★ ★ ★ ★ ★ ★ ★ ★ ★ ★ ★ ★ ★ ★

Zachary Taylor became a war hero during the Mexican War and later served as the twelfth president of the United States.

Growing Up in the West

No president of the United States came to office with as little political experience as Zachary Taylor. Before being elected the nation's twelfth president, Taylor served his country as a soldier for forty years and became a national hero in the **Mexican War** (1846–1848). Taylor's fame as a soldier helped him win the presidency, yet he was indifferent to politics for most of his life and had never voted in a presidential election.

Nevertheless, as president, Taylor displayed courage and boldness in office. Some admiring historians believe that had he lived long enough to serve out his term, the actions of this president may have prevented the Civil War, the bloodiest in this nation's history.

A Prominent Virginia Family

Zachary Taylor was born on November 24, 1784, near Barboursville, Virginia, the third son of Richard Taylor and Sarah Dabney Strother Taylor. The Taylors, one of Virginia's most prominent families, owned a large plantation in the Tidewater region of Virginia. Both sides of Taylor's family had been in America for generations. One of Zachary's maternal ancestors, William Brewster, had come to America on the *Mayflower* with the other Pilgrims in 1620. James Madison, the country's fourth president, was Zachary's second cousin. Zachary was

Zachary Taylor came from a family of notable figures, such as President James Madison, his second cousin.

also related to the Revolutionary War hero Henry Lee and the Civil War general Robert E. Lee.

Zachary's father, Richard Taylor, had served as an officer in the American Revolution. By the war's end, he held the rank of colonel. For his service, Taylor was rewarded with six thousand acres of land in the Kentucky Territory. Like hundreds of other Virginians and Carolinians, Taylor decided to leave his plantation, its soil depleted by years of tobacco growing, and move to Kentucky with his family to start a new life. Because his wife was pregnant at the time with Zachary, Richard left her and their two sons at the home of Colonel Valentine Johnson, near Barboursville, Virginia, and traveled to Kentucky alone to claim his land and clear it for a homestead. Richard returned when Zachary was eight months old, and the following spring the family moved to the Kentucky wilderness. In due time, Richard became a respected public servant in Kentucky, which became the fifteenth state in 1792. He served as a collector of the port of Louisville, as a delegate to Kentucky's State Constitutional Convention, and four times as a presidential elector in the **electoral college**.

Growing Up in Kentucky

Richard Taylor built a log cabin for his family on Beargrass Creek, two miles from the Ohio River. He later built a large brick house on the site, where the couple raised six more children. Although the town of Louisville was only five miles to the west, the Taylors lived in a wilderness surrounded by wild animals and American Indians. One day Zachary and his brothers were playing with some boys in the woods and then parted. Later that same day, the boys were found murdered and scalped near where the Taylors had left them, presumably by hostile Indians.

Little is known of Zachary's childhood. As a youth, he performed chores, hunted for raccoons and deer, and rode horseback along wooded trails. He did not see the inside of a schoolroom until he was in his teens and then only briefly. There were few schools on the Kentucky frontier. Zachary was taught by visiting tutors that his father hired occasionally. One of these tutors, Elisha Ayer of Connecticut, later recalled that Zachary was a bright and good student. The school Zachary later attended was run by a local man named Kean O'Hara.

A Soldier's Life

Until the age of twenty-three, Zachary remained at home and helped his father and brothers run the family plantation. Zachary's older brother William was a lieutenant in the U.S. Army, and Zachary also aspired to become a soldier. After spending a short time in the Kentucky **militia**, where he was exposed to the adventure and discipline of the soldier's life, he became determined to make a career in the army. A cousin, James Taylor, wrote him a letter of recommendation to James Madison, then

Young Taylor spent many hours helping his family with daily chores.

secretary of state in the administration of President Thomas Jefferson. Madison's influence got Taylor, his second cousin, a commission as a first lieutenant of infantry on May 3, 1808.

Taylor's first assignment was to recruit soldiers for the Seventh Infantry Regiment in Kentucky. In April 1809, Lieutenant Taylor and eighty men traveled down the Mississippi River to New Orleans to report to General James Wilkinson, commander of federal troops in the new Louisiana Territory, recently purchased from France.

ROMANCE AND MARRIAGE

While Taylor was in New Orleans, a deadly **malaria** epidemic struck the city. Out of a garrison of 2,000 soldiers, 686 died from disease and fatigue. Taylor caught malaria but survived. He was sent home on leave in 1810 to recover.

The Post-Revolutionary U.S. Army

When Zachary Taylor was commissioned in the U.S. Army it was not a prestigious institution. Many Americans in the days after the Revolution looked on the military with disdain and suspicion. The highly organized army of the British was still hated for trying to defeat the rebellious colonists in the Revolutionary War. In a letter to his wife in 1802, Secretary of the Treasury  Albert Gallatin referred to the American military as "our little army" and called it a "perhaps unnecessary evil." With peacetime, the army's main job was to build and inhabit forts across the wilderness and protect settlers there from hostile Indians. It could be dull and thankless work. Many officers were incompetent and corrupt, perhaps none more so than Taylor's first commander, General James Wilkinson (above), who had been implicated in the conspiracy of the former vice president Aaron Burr to seize territory from the Spanish and establish a republic in the Southwest. Wilkinson had been acquitted of the charges against him in a court-martial, but a cloud of suspicion still hung over him. Life in these frontier outposts could be filled with boredom, and the soldiers, with little to do, often squabbled among themselves. One of Taylor's first assignments was to Fort Knox in Tennessee to replace a commander who had shot and killed a lieutenant he had had a running quarrel with.

MALARIA AND YELLOW FEVER

Now largely a matter of concern only in the tropics, malaria, a dreaded disease known since ancient times, is caused by a parasite that lives in certain mosquitoes and is transmitted to humans by their bite. The victim suffers regular attacks of chills and fever that last two or more hours. Some forms of malaria are deadlier than others. Louisiana, with its tropical climate, is one of the few states in the United States where malaria was a problem. Yellow fever, another deadly disease spread by mosquitoes, had also been a killer in the state for centuries. In 1853, when more than 12,000 people died of yellow fever in New Orleans, Louisiana's death rate was the highest of any American state in the nineteenth century. The Louisiana State Board of Public Health was established in 1855, the first of its kind in the United States. Forty-two years later, in 1897, a doctor in India discovered that mosquitoes spread malaria.

While visiting the home of a neighbor, Samuel Chews, Taylor met Chews's visiting sister-in-law, Margaret Mackall Smith. The two fell in love and after a whirlwind courtship were married on June 21, 1810. Zachary was twenty-five and his bride twenty-one. Richard Taylor gave the newlyweds 324 acres of land to farm and build a home on. The following spring, the couple had their first child, a daughter, Ann.

In 1811 Great Britain's continuing **impressment** of American merchant sailors for service in the Royal Navy's **men-of-war** led to the outbreak of the War of 1812, the first of four wars that Taylor participated in.

MARGARET TAYLOR

Some president's wives have been reluctant first ladies, perhaps none more so than Margaret Mackall Smith Taylor. Born on September 21, 1788, in Calvert County, Maryland, she lost her mother at an early age, and her father, a plantation owner, died soon after. A deeply religious woman, Margaret, known as Peggy, was also a courageous one. She followed her husband fearlessly, with their children in tow,

to many a distant military outpost. "My wife was as much a soldier as I was," Zachary Taylor was proud of saying in later life.

Margaret did not want her famous husband to be president and prayed fervently that the Democratic candidate, Lewis Cass, would win the election of 1848. When Zachary won, she resigned herself to being first lady but did little actively in the role. She spent most of her time in the White House knitting in her second-floor room while her youngest daughter, Mary, took over the White House hosting duties.

After the sudden death of her husband, Margaret returned with their children to Louisville, where she taught Sunday school regularly. She spent her last years living with her daughter Mary in Louisiana and surrounded by her grandchildren. She died at age sixty-three of a fever.

During the War of 1812 Tecumseh, chief of the Shawnee tribe, allied with the British.

Indian Fighter

*I*n the spring of 1811, Taylor was promoted to captain and sent to Fort Knox in the Indiana Territory. His assignment was to repair the fort and defend the area's settlers from Indian attacks, a typical order of the day for the military.

On June 19, 1812, the rising tensions between Great Britain and the United States erupted into war. Many native tribes sided with the British in the **War of 1812** because they promised their Indian allies the return of their lands taken by the Americans if they prevailed. British troops, pouring down from British-held Canada, joined their Indian allies in seizing American forts.

The Defense of Fort Harrison

Taylor was sent to take command of Fort Harrison, in the Indiana Territory on the Wabash River. About eleven o'clock on the evening of September 4, 1812, he was awakened by the cries of his men. A force of 450 Indians led by the Shawnee chief Tecumseh attacked the fort and set the **blockhouse** on fire. Taylor had only fifty men in the fort, many of them ill with fever. Taylor kept a cool head. He ordered those soldiers healthy enough to fight to take their posts; the others he had tear down the roof of the **blockhouse** in order to put out the blaze. The fighting continued until morning, when the Indians fled. Seeing the stiff resistance they faced, they did not return. "Nothing saved the fort but the presence of mind, courage, prudence and energy of the commander. . . ." wrote the historian Benson Lossing.

Taylor's brave defense of Fort Harrison won him widespread praise. By the time the war ended in early 1815, he was

TECUMSEH

The Shawnee warrior and orator Tecumseh is one of the most renowned American Indian leaders. Tecumseh was born in 1768 near present-day Dayton, Ohio. White settlers killed both his father and an older brother. When Tecumseh, whose name in Shawnee means "shooting star," became a chief, he came up with an ambitious plan to defeat the settlers in their westward expansion. He envisioned a great alliance of many Indians to fight the Americans. Together with his younger brother, Tenskwatawa, known as the

TECUMSEH

Prophet, Tecumseh traveled from the Great Lakes region to the Gulf of Mexico, speaking before one tribe after another to persuade them to join his alliance. Whatever hopes he had were dashed when William Henry Harrison, the governor of the Indiana Territory, defeated his forces and destroyed Tenskwatawa's village at the Battle of Tippecanoe in 1811. After the outbreak of the War of 1812, Tecumseh allied himself with the British, who made him a brigadier general. Tecumseh and his Indian forces took part in numerous battles, including the taking of Detroit and an unsuccessful attack on Fort Harrison. Tecumseh died in Canada at the Battle of the Thames River in 1813. His dream of an American Indian alliance died with him.

promoted to the rank of **brevet** major. He was one of the first American officers to be awarded this rank.

A Brief Retirement

With the end of the War of 1812, the government drastically reduced the size of the army from a force of 60,000 men to 10,000. With fewer officers needed, Taylor became a captain again. He requested another promotion but was refused. Angry at this treatment, Taylor resigned and returned to Louisville to farm his plantation.

"I have commenced making corn and tobacco & am now in my own cabbin [sic]," Taylor wrote to a relative. "I do not regret the change of calling I have pursued." Taylor was not cut out to be a farmer, however. He missed the army. When he was offered the rank of major in 1816, he returned to service. On the day he was given his new assignment, August 16, his third daughter, Octavia, was born. For the next sixteen years Taylor commanded forts on the frontier in the territories of Arkansas, Missouri, Wisconsin, Michigan, Oklahoma, and Louisiana. His wife and children joined him in Louisiana in 1819; that same year he was promoted to lieutenant colonel.

Taylor was impressed by the rich soil of Louisiana and decided to establish a home and plantation there. The hot, humid climate bred disease, however, and in 1820, Octavia contracted malaria and died at age three. Less than four months later, Margaret, the youngest child, died of the same disease. Mrs. Taylor also contracted the disease but survived. Taylor refused to let these tragedies drive him from Louisiana. He bought and settled on a five-hundred-acre cotton plantation forty miles north of the city of Baton Rouge.

Taylor returned to active service in the U.S. army after taking a break at the end of the War of 1812.

The Indian Removal Act

By 1820 the number of Americans living west of the Appalachian Mountains was about equal to the population of the original thirteen states at the time of the American Revolution. These pioneers included families and individuals, rich and poor. They came looking for land to clear and to establish homes, farms, and a new life. Their West was not the West of the present day; it was the land between the Appalachians and the Mississippi River—primarily Indiana and Ohio in the north, Kentucky and Tennessee in the central region, and Alabama and Mississippi farther south. Most of these lands were already inhabited by Native American tribes who had lived there for hundreds of years. A number of southern Indians had already been persuaded by the U.S. government to move to the so-called Indian country, in what is present-day Arkansas. However, in 1830, 120,000 Indians still occupied a considerable territory in four southern states, including parts of Florida and Georgia.

The Indian Removal Act, passed by Congress in 1830, gave the government the authority to forcibly remove Indians from their homelands in the Southeast and move them west of the Mississippi. The tribes who agreed to go peaceably were given money for their lands, free transportation, and new land in Indian Territory, a region of variable size occupying much of present-day Oklahoma. The journey was long and arduous for the Indians, and sometimes they were given tainted meat to eat on the way. The Removal Act led to two conflicts with Indians who either refused to move or changed their minds after removal. Zachary Taylor played a major role in both of these conflicts.

Black Hawk War

Among the resettled tribes were the Sauk and Fox peoples of northwestern Illinois, who had agreed to relocate in new land farther west in Iowa. Life there was difficult for them, however, as it was for many other relocated tribes. Food was scarce, and they had to contend with their enemy the Sioux, who already occupied the region. In April 1832, the aged Sauk chief Black Hawk led a force of between four hundred and five hundred men across the Mississippi River back into Illinois and attacked and killed white settlers.

Taylor was ordered to capture Black Hawk and pursued him for months across the Wisconsin Territory. On August 1–2, 1832, he finally caught up with the Indians at the Mississippi River. In the Battle of Bad Axe, the army suffered twenty-seven casualties, the Indians nearly four times as many. When Black Hawk, who survived the fight and fled, later surrendered to Taylor on August 27 at Fort du Chien, the four-month conflict came to an end.

Taylor had a deep sympathy for the plight of Native Americans. He complained to the War Department about settlers and miners invading territory set aside for the Indians and requested from the secretary of war authority to "burn and destroy the establishments of all squatters together with every description of property and to remove them, and all other whites who may attempt to trespass, encroach or enter upon the Indian Territory." From 1834 to 1836, Taylor even built a school where Winnebago Indians could be educated.

One of the two officers put in charge of the prisoner Black Hawk was Jefferson Davis, a Kentuckian and West Point graduate. Davis had earlier fallen in love with Taylor's eighteen-year-old

Sauk chief Black Hawk, angry with the Indian Removal Act, led his warriors on a rampage in 1832, killing and attacking white settlers.

American Indians, led by Black Hawk, were killed in the Battle of Bad Axe as they tried to cross the Mississippi River into an area they were originally driven from.

daughter Sarah Knox, but Taylor refused to give his consent to their marriage. He felt, on the basis of his own family's experience, that the cost to any woman who married a soldier was too high. Davis was promoted and transferred to the Southwest for two years, but his love for Knox, as the family called her, did not fade, nor did hers for him. In June 1835, Davis resigned from the army and shortly after married Knox, with her parents' reluctant consent. The newlyweds traveled down the Mississippi River to honeymoon at Brierfield, Davis's island plantation near Vicksburg, Mississippi. During that time, they both caught malaria. Davis recovered, but Knox did not; she died less than three months after their wedding. Davis was devastated and went into seclusion.

Jefferson Davis

After the death of his wife, Jefferson Davis became wealthy running his Mississippi plantation. He remarried in 1845 and the same year was elected to a Democratic seat in the U.S. House of Representatives. He resigned his seat to fight in the Mexican War; he commanded a Mississippi regiment and served under his former father-in-law, Zachary Taylor. Davis's valor and skill at the battles of Monterrey and Buena Vista made him a war hero. After the war, he was appointed U.S. senator from Mississippi on the death of the elected senator. In the Senate he supported states' rights and slavery; he resigned his seat in 1851 and ran, unsuccessfully, for governor of Mississippi. He served as secretary of war under President Franklin Pierce from 1853 to 1857 and then returned to the Senate. When the southern states seceded, the new confederacy elected him their president. When the war ended in southern defeat, Davis was arrested on charges of treason and spent two years in prison awaiting trial, which never took place. He was finally released in 1867. He spent his last years defending his actions during the war and writing a book about it. Jefferson Davis, the Confederacy's first and only president, died on December 6, 1889, at age eighty-one.

The Second Seminole War

Following the Black Hawk War, Taylor returned to his previous post at Fort Crawford, at Prairie du Chien in the Michigan Territory. During the next five years, he spent most of his time building roads through the wilderness and training new troops.

Then in 1837 the Seminole tribe of Florida, defeated by General Andrew Jackson back in 1817, went to war again to drive out the growing number of settlers. Taylor was ordered to Florida in 1837 to put down the uprising. With a force of one thousand men he marched east from Tampa Bay into the Seminoles' territory.

The Seminoles

Though not as well known as the wars involving the Plains Indians, the Second Seminole War was, in the words of the historian John S. D. Eisenhower, "one of the . . . costliest and most frustrating 'wars' the United States Army ever fought against the various Native American tribes." The war cost $20 million, and some 1,500 soldiers lost their lives.

The Seminoles displayed an extraordinary determination. Even after the death of their war leader Osceola in 1838, they continued to fight. The Seminoles were finally defeated in 1842, and more than four thousand captured Seminoles were sent west to live. Other tribal members, too weak to fight, disappeared into the most remote parts of the Everglades, where they continued to live free. The Seminoles are the only Indian nation that never surrendered to the United States.

Colonel Zachary Taylor and his men defeat the Seminoles at Lake Okeechobee in Florida in 1837.

On Christmas Day 1837, Taylor met a force of seven hundred Indians at Lake Okeechobee. The soldiers had to pass through tangled weeds and mud to reach the enemy. The mud was so deep that they had to dismount from their horses and wade through the mire on foot. The first line was composed of volunteers. When their commander was shot dead by the Seminoles, the volunteers broke ranks and fled. The regular soldiers behind them marched forward. The fighting was fierce and bloody, but in three hours the Seminoles were forced back and fled into the swamps. The victory of the Battle of Okeechobee was the most decisive battle of the Second Seminole War, but as Taylor himself admitted, his victory came at a high price. Some 26 of his men were killed and 112 wounded.

The Not-So-Well-Dressed Officer

Never one for formality and protocol, Zachary Taylor was one of the most eccentric officers in the U.S. Army in terms of his dress. Even when promoted to general he favored wide-brimmed straw hats rather than regulation headgear and preferred comfortable coats and trousers, often unmatched, to his uniform. In the field, he looked more like a farmer or a camp follower than a commanding officer. One freshly appointed lieutenant took him for exactly that and called him an "old codger." When he later learned of his mistake, he apologized at length to Taylor. Taylor simply smiled and told the young officer, "Never judge a stranger by his clothes."

Taylor was then put in charge of all army troops in Florida and pursued the Seminoles with a steely determination. "We must abandon general operations and confine ourselves to minute and specific ones," Taylor declared. He divided the state into a grid of squares, each twenty miles on a side, and patrolled them thoroughly. Taylor brought in thirty-three Cuban bloodhounds to hunt down the fleeing Seminoles. Fearing the bloodhounds would attack the defenseless Seminoles, the American public called the tactic inhumane and condemned it. The bloodhounds failed to find any Indians, in any event, and led the soldiers on a wild goose chase.

The war dragged on for seven years owing to the elusiveness of the Seminoles. Taylor, who spent two years in Florida, looked on his time there with some regret. He later called it a "miserable country . . . where an officer who has any regard for honesty, truth, or humanity, has but little to gain, and everything to lose." Nevertheless, his dogged efforts against the Seminoles earned him a promotion to brevet brigadier general and a new nickname, Old Rough and Ready.

Around the time this portrait was painted, Zachary Taylor was the army's commander of the southern division.

AT WAR WITH MEXICO

*I*n 1841 Zachary Taylor was made commander of the U.S. Army's southern division, which included parts of Louisiana, Arkansas, and the Oklahoma Territory. He set up his headquarters at Fort Smith, Arkansas, and moved his family to a plantation he bought north of Baton Rouge, Louisiana, for $95,000. During the next three years, Taylor divided his time between building forts in the region and inspecting existing forts. An overseer ran his plantation, which include a number of slaves.

PREPARING FOR WAR

Texas, once part of Mexico, had declared its independence as a free republic in 1836. The majority of white settlers were ready

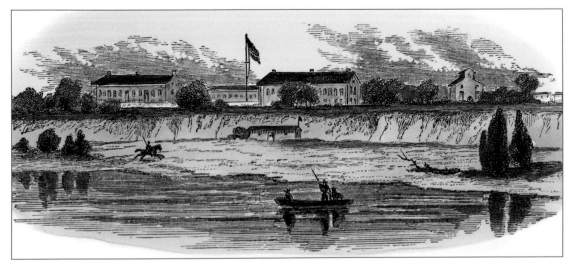

Fort Smith in Arkansas served as Commander Taylor's headquarters.

Zachary Taylor, Slaveholder

Eight presidents held slaves while they were in office; Taylor was the last of them. He owned 118 slaves when he was elected president and acquired 64 more slaves just weeks before his death. Taylor treated his slaves well and once had his overseer divide up $500 at Christmas among them for good conduct during the year. Despite this benevolence, Taylor, unlike George Washington, did not free his slaves at his death; neither did he seek as president to end slavery in the fifteen southern states where it existed. He felt strongly, however, that slavery should not extend to new territories and states. This stance put him at odds with many southern legislators as well as some in the North who believed in popular sovereignty, the theory that each new territory or state had the right to decide whether to allow slavery or not.

and eager by the early 1840s to join the United States. As the movement to annex Texas grew, tensions with Mexico grew as well. The Mexicans feared that if Texas became part of the United States, the Americans would invade other parts of the Mexican Southwest. They threatened to go to war over the issue.

The U.S. War Department put the army on alert, and in June 1844, General Taylor was sent to Fort Jesup, located on the border between Louisiana and Texas, with a force called the Army of Observation.

In the spring of 1845, Taylor was ordered to move his troops farther south to the mouth of the Nueces River near the trading post of Corpus Christi, Texas. He had under his command four thousand men, half of the entire U.S. Army. Negotiations between Texas and the United States concluded, and on December 29, Texas was admitted as the twenty-eighth state. The Rio Grande, a river, was established as the new border between Texas and Mexico. The Mexicans objected and threatened to attack. President James Polk sent Taylor and his troops to the Rio Grande to establish a defensive post at Point Isabel and another post eighteen miles inland along the river opposite the Mexican city of Matamoras. Taylor arrived at Matamoras on March 28, 1846, and was soon met by a large Mexican force. The Mexican troops watched in silence as Taylor ordered the building of Fort Brown, which is the site of present-day Brownsville, Texas.

On April 12, the Mexican commander, General Pedro de Ampudia, sent a message warning the Americans to retreat within twenty-four hours or face attack. Taylor refused to budge. Captain Seth Thornton led a scouting party along the northern side of the Rio Grande. On April 24 or 25, close to two thousand Mexicans ambushed Thornton and his men and killed or captured all sixty-three of them. Taylor sent a dispatch to President Polk telling him hostilities had begun. It was the unofficial start of the Mexican War.

Two Victories

Taylor marched his men to Fort Texas, which was being bombarded by Mexican troops. Prevented from reaching the fort, Taylor turned north to Palo Alto. There the Americans were fired upon by a line of Mexican cannon under the direction of General Mariano Arista. Taylor responded by firing his own cannon, which were superior to those of the Mexicans, and

The Battle of Palo Alto, led by Taylor, was the first battle of the Mexican War.

drove the enemy back. Despite being outnumbered three to one, the Americans won the Battle of Palo Alto; American casualties included only nine soldiers killed and forty-five wounded. On the other side, more than two hundred Mexicans were killed and four hundred wounded. It was the first battle of the war and a shining victory for Taylor.

The Mexican army retreated to Resaca de la Palma, a scrubland with thick underbrush where Arista figured the American artillery would be useless. Taylor disregarded the Mexican firing line and plunged into battle. He sent a small group with Captain Charles May to capture the Mexican cannon. They not only captured the cannon but also General Díaz de la Vega, the Mexican field commander.

The fighting continued for two hours; then the Mexicans broke rank and fled for the banks of the Rio Grande. Many tried to swim across the river and drowned. Mexican casualties were five hundred, nearly five times that of the Americans. In just two days Taylor had scored two military victories and was hailed back home in the United States as a hero. Congress praised his skill and bravery, while Louisiana lawmakers appropriated $500 to buy him a new sword to replace one lost in battle.

President Polk had earlier made General Winfield Scott supreme commander of the war with Mexico. However, when given the order from Polk to advance, Scott ignored it and spent the summer organizing and training troops in Washington. Polk was unhappy with Scott and decided to make Taylor, after his recent victories, his new war commander.

THE BATTLE OF MONTERREY

Taylor faced serious challenges as he prepared to advance north to Mexico's largest northern city, Monterrey. Thousands of his soldiers had died from dysentery, a disease spread through bad drinking water. The militiamen and short-term volunteers who joined him as reinforcements were undisciplined and inexperienced. With about 6,600 troops, half of them volunteers, Taylor advanced toward Monterrey in September 1846. Waiting for him there were 7,300 Mexican soldiers under the command of General Pedro de Ampudia. The city, with four forts, was well defended. Taylor reached Monterrey on September 21 and divided his army into two. One flank, led by Brigadier General William Worth, attacked Independence Hill. The other flank attacked Fort Teneria to the east. Three days of bloody fighting ensued.

OLD WHITEY

General Taylor rode into battle during the Mexican War on his favorite horse, Old Whitey. Few presidents have been as attached to a horse as Taylor was to his. His inaugural invitation bore an elaborate picture of himself and Old Whitey. When Taylor was president, Whitey was allowed to graze on the White House lawn. Visitors would often attempt to pluck souvenir hairs from his tail. Old Whitey was a lively horse and would perk  up and prance whenever he heard parade music.

Old Whitey outlived his master. At Taylor's funeral, in accord with long-standing military tradition, the horse was led riderless behind his master's casket with a pair of Taylor's boots turned around in the saddle's stirrups.

The two halves of the American army drove the Mexicans into their last stronghold, the center of the city. Taylor entered the city with his men and fought the Mexicans door-to-door in hand-to-hand combat. One volunteer wrote in a letter home, "I was within ten feet of General Taylor. . . . He was cool as a cucumber and ordered us to pass into the city and break open the houses. God knows how any of us got out." The Americans occupied the residence of the local bishop, on Independence Hill. The morning of September 24, General Ampudia surrendered to Taylor at his headquarters. Although he had won, Taylor and his men were exhausted and needed to rest and reorganize. Because of the exhaustion and Ampudia's promise that Mexico sought peace and an end to war, Taylor was generous in his terms. He allowed the Mexicans to leave freely and head south and said he would agree to an eight-week **armistice**. He hoped that by then the Mexicans would be ready to surrender.

After the Battle of Monterrery, Mexico surrendered to General Taylor.

When Polk heard of the armistice, he was furious. He had expected Taylor to crush the Mexican army and bring the war to a quick end. He sent orders for the general to end the cease-fire, but the order arrived only two weeks before the eight weeks were up and had little effect. Taylor came up with a plan to march from Vera Cruz, on the Mexican coast, inland to Mexico City, the capital. Polk approved the plan but chose Winfield Scott, who he now favored, to carry it out. Taylor was also ordered to give up nine thousand troops to Scott for his march to Mexico City.

Scott sent Taylor, whom he was on friendly terms with, a nicely worded but patronizing letter. ". . . my dear General," wrote Scott, "I shall be obliged to take from you most of the gallant officers and men . . . whom you have so long and so nobly commanded. . . . But I rely on your patriotism to submit to the temporary sacrifice with cheerfulness."

Taylor was anything but cheerful at being passed over for this important campaign but being a good soldier, he obeyed orders.

Victory at Buena Vista

Taylor had orders from the War Department to stay put in Monterrey, but he did not follow them. In January 1847 he moved his remaining troops southwest from Monterrey to the town of Agua Neuva. Unbeknownst to him, the Mexican leader Antonio López de Santa Anna was moving north to attack him.

Santa Anna, the victor at the Alamo in 1836 and the former Mexican president, had been exiled from Mexico, but the war's upheaval gave him a chance to return and regain power. President Polk had given Santa Anna safe passage to Mexico City after the former dictator promised he would help negotiate a

Winfield Scott: Old Fuss and Feathers

Zachary Taylor and Winfield Scott, the leading military men of their day, were markedly different in style and character. Taylor was largely uneducated; Scott had gone to William and Mary College, in Virginia, and studied law before joining the army in 1808. Taylor's disheveled dress and deportment were unmilitary and eccentric, while Scott's love of colorful regimental uniforms earned him the nickname Old Fuss and Feathers.

Before the Mexican War, Scott's star shone brighter than Taylor's. His service in the War of 1812 made him a national hero and earned him a special congressional medal. By 1841 Scott was general-in-chief of the U.S. Army.

After the Mexican War, Taylor and Scott, rivals on the battlefield, became rivals in politics. Like Taylor, Scott aspired to be president and vied with him for the **Whig** nomination in 1848, which Taylor won. Four years later, Scott secured the Whig nomination for president but lost in the election to the **Democrat** Franklin Pierce. If Scott and Taylor shared anything, it was their loyalty to the Union. When Virginia, Scott's home state, seceded from the Union, he refused to join the Confederacy. He retired from the army in 1861, soon after the outbreak of the Civil War, and died five years later, a Union man to the end.

peace with the Americans. Instead the wily general took command of the Mexican army and set out to fight his country's enemy.

On February 19, scouts reported to Taylor that an army of 15,000 soldiers led by Santa Anna was approaching. The general ordered the army to move to a better defensive position north at the **hacienda** of Buena Vista, which was surrounded by mountains. Santa Anna sent a message to Taylor urging him to surrender to his vastly superior force and be treated "with the consideration belonging to the Mexican character." Taylor responded: "In reply to your note of this date summoning me to surrender my forces at discretion, I beg leave to say that I decline acceding to your request."

Santa Anna's army actually numbered only 4,760 men, but it still outnumbered Taylor's force four to one. The Mexicans advanced, and the battle began in earnest on February 23. Taylor had left the main army to secure his supply depot at Saltillo to the north. Meanwhile, his main army was starting to give way under the Mexican onslaught. Taylor rushed back to the field with reinforcements. His bravery in the face of death inspired his men to fight on despite the odds. Bullets whizzed through Taylor's coat and sleeve as he cried out orders and words of encouragement. As the battle raged around him, Taylor remained calm, standing at one point behind the flying artillery of Captain Braxton Bragg. "A little more grape[shot], Captain Bragg, a great deal more grape!" he was heard to say. At one point, a subordinate came to Taylor and announced, "General, we are whipped." To which Taylor replied, "That is for me to determine." Among the officers who distinguished themselves that day were William T. Sherman, who would become an important Union general in the Civil War, and Taylor's former son-in-law Jefferson Davis, who fought all day with a foot wound. Not all Taylor's men stood the course; 267 were killed, 456 were wounded, and 23 were

Taylor's successful campaign throughout Mexico continued at the Battle of Buena Vista, his last battle in the war.

missing in action, but 1,500 deserted the field. Mexican losses were far greater; after losing 1,800 men, Santa Anna retreated in defeat.

Buena Vista was Taylor's final battle as a soldier and his finest hour. His victory against overwhelming odds made him a national hero despite Polk's criticism that his victory was a costly one in human life. Taylor countered that it was the government's fault his army was small and vulnerable to attack. In a letter he said he would look to his reward "to the consciousness of pure motives, and to the final verdict of impartial history." In September 1847 Winfield Scott marched into Mexico City, and the war ended in American victory. By then, Zachary Taylor had taken his leave of Mexico and was back home in Louisiana.

Whig Party leaders thought that Taylor's exploits would make him a strong candidate in the 1848 presidential election. Taylor initially scoffed at the idea, but when the rumor became a reality, he decided to run.

The Whig Party favored Zachary Taylor as its candidate for president, as can be seen in this election poster from 1848.

THE SOLDIER-PRESIDENT

On his return to Louisiana, Taylor was hailed as a national hero. At that time in American history, military men were perhaps the most admired of national figures. Taylor's unlikely victory at Buena Vista against tremendous odds captured the imagination of the nation. Old Rough and Ready was the man of the hour.

A PRESIDENTIAL HOPEFUL

The Whig Party had formed in 1834 to oppose the policies of President Andrew Jackson and his Democratic Party. Jackson increased the power of the executive branch, and the Whigs wanted to reduce it and give more power to Congress, the legislative branch. They also favored economic protectionism for American business and industry and supported a high **tariff** on foreign goods. The first Whig president was William Henry Harrison, another military hero, elected in 1840. Harrison died of pneumonia barely a month after becoming president at age sixty-eight. John Tyler, his vice president, who had originally been a Democrat, succeeded Harrison and upset the Whigs by repudiating their policies. They quickly disassociated themselves from him. After yet another Democratic presidency, that of James Polk, the Whigs were anxious to regain the White House and saw Taylor as their most electable candidate.

Taylor had no political experience, a fact the Whigs believed was in his favor. His views on controversial issues were unknown, and he had no enemies in Congress. His reputation as a down-to-earth man of the people made him tremendously popular with the public. In addition, he could appeal to people in both the North and the South. Northerners liked him as a military hero and national figure. Southerners admired him as one of their own, a Southerner by birth and a slaveholder.

The question was, would Taylor, who had spent nearly his entire career in the army, be interested in the presidential nomination? During his six months of leave, the general began to get a taste of his great popularity and enjoyed it. In December 1847, a group of young Whig congressmen, including Abraham Lincoln of Illinois, formed a Taylor-for-president club and called themselves the Young Indians. If the politicians and newspapers believed he was presidential material, Taylor thought, then perhaps he was. He certainly felt he could fill the office better than Polk, who was not running for a second term. However, Taylor made it clear he would not actively seek the nomination. If elected, he wrote, "it must be by the spontaneous move of the people, & not by any agency of mine . . . as I am not at all anxious for the office under any circumstances, & will be the president of all the people if at all, & not of a party." Nevertheless, in April 1848, Taylor officially announced his availability to run as a Whig candidate.

THE WHIG CONVENTION

There were other candidates for the presidential nomination when the Whigs convened in Philadelphia for their national convention in June 1848. Heading the list were the leading Whig senators, Henry Clay and Daniel Webster. Both men had run for president before and failed to win the nomination. They also had, over time, cultivated many enemies in Congress. Another potential

Abraham Lincoln: Congressman

By many accounts, the best speech of the presidential campaign of 1848 was given by the Illinois congressman Abraham Lincoln. At that time, prior to the birth of the Republican Party, Lincoln was a Whig.

On July 27, 1848, Lincoln delivered a compelling, often humorous speech in the House of Representatives on Taylor's behalf that made a virtue out of his refusal to take a firm stand on most issues. "If you desire a bank, an alteration of the tariff, internal improvements, any or all, I will not hinder you," said Lincoln, speaking for Taylor. "If you do not desire them, I will not attempt to force them on you. . . ." Lincoln also made fun of the Democratic candidate, Lewis Cass, whose modest military career he compared to his own minor service in the Black Hawk War. "If General Cass went in advance of me in picking huckleberries, I guess I surpassed him in charges upon the wild onions," Lincoln declared. The speech brought great fame to the thirty-nine-year-old congressman, who would one day himself be president.

candidate was Winfield Scott, the other hero of the Mexican War. For all his success as a military man, Scott was not as well liked by the public as Taylor, and his candidacy soon fizzled. On the first **ballot**, Taylor led with 111 votes to Clay's 97, with Scott and Webster trailing far behind. On the fourth ballot, Taylor won the nomination with a majority of 171 votes. Millard Fillmore, a former congressman and the **comptroller** of New York State, was chosen as the vice presidential nominee.

Clay's disappointment turned to animosity toward Taylor and his candidacy. He refused to support him in the election or vote for him.

The Whig leaders sent a letter to Taylor at his home in Baton Rouge to inform him that he was their presidential candidate. Taylor, who had become tired of paying for mail with insufficient postage or no postage at all sent to him by his many admirers, refused to pay for the letter. It was promptly sent off, unopened, to the dead-letter office along with his other unwanted mail. When a few weeks passed

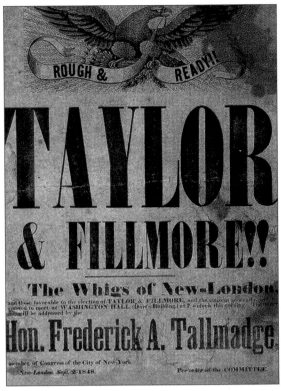

A broadside announces a Whig campaign rally for Taylor and Fillmore during the 1848 presidential election campaign.

and the Whigs had not heard from their nominee, they sent off another letter, this one prepaid. Taylor received it, read it, and immediately sent his acceptance.

Back in May, the Democrats had nominated the Michigan senator Lewis Cass at their convention in Baltimore, Maryland. Cass, the first Democratic candidate from what was then the American Northwest, had served in the War of 1812 and as Andrew Jackson's secretary of war. His running mate, General William O. Butler of Kentucky, had served under Taylor at the

Battle of Monterrey. A former congressman, Butler had also served as **aide-de-camp** to General Andrew Jackson at the Battle of New Orleans during the War of 1812.

LEWIS CASS

In many ways, the Democratic presidential candidate in 1848, Lewis Cass, was far better qualified to be president than Zachary Taylor. As governor of the Michigan Territory (1813–1831), Cass had acquired experience governing a region that was later carved up into four states—Michigan, Wisconsin, Iowa, and Minnesota. After serving five years as President Jackson's secretary of war, Cass was appointed minister to France. After losing the election of 1848, Cass returned to the Senate, where he served from 1849 to 1857. That year he became President James Buchanan's secretary of state. Although a strong spokesman throughout his career for popular sovereignty, Cass was discouraged by Buchanan's soft policies toward the South and resigned from his cabinet in 1860, with the outbreak of the Civil War only a year away. An admired statesman, Cass retired from public life and died in 1866.

A Three-Way Race

Slavery was the most divisive issue in the country. Taylor's views on this and other issues were unknown even to the Whigs who nominated him. Cass, unlike Taylor, openly supported popular sovereignty. Slavery and popular sovereignty were pressing issues because the United States had just gained the territories of California and New Mexico (including present-day Arizona) from Mexico under the **Treaty of Guadalupe Hidalgo**, which ended the Mexican War.

Democrats who opposed slavery and its expansion left the convention unhappy with Cass's nomination. They decided to form their own party, which they called the Free Soil Party. The new party, whose slogan was "Free Soil, Free Speech, Free Labor, Free Men," chose the former Democratic president Martin Van Buren, who had lost his bid for reelection to Harrison eight years earlier, as its presidential candidate. The Free Soilers picked former president John Quincy Adams's son Charles Francis Adams, who had been a Whig, as Van Buren's running mate.

The campaign had its share of personal attacks. Democrats branded Taylor a "military **autocrat**" and a slave master, uneducated, and semi-illiterate. The Whigs called Cass "a sly, artful, intriguing politician." In 1848 the Whigs proved themselves masterful campaigners, as they had in the 1840 Harrison campaign, when they'd set up Harrison "log cabin clubs"—even though Harrison, who was well-to-do, had not been born in a log cabin. For the Taylor campaign they established "Rough and Ready clubs" across the nation and organized colorful parades and rallies for their candidate. Tuneful ditties, such as "Old

VICE PRESIDENT MILLARD FILLMORE

Despite his relative obscurity, Millard Fillmore was chosen to run for vice president because the Whigs felt his long career in New York politics would help them win this most important electorate state.

Born into a poor farming family with nine children in upstate New York, Fillmore worked his way up from apprentice to a cloth maker to schoolteacher to lawyer. He was first elected to the state legislature in 1828 and to the U.S. Congress in 1832.

Upon retiring from Congress in 1843, he seemed destined for oblivion. He failed to win the Whig vice presidential nomination in 1844 and lost the election for governor of New York as the Whig candidate the same year. His election to the office of state comptroller in 1847 might have been the end of his career if not for his surprise selection as vice presidential nominee.

Fillmore had little in common politically with the president he served. As vice president, Fillmore presided over the often raucous Senate debates on the Compromise of 1850. While he was in favor of the compromise bill, he made no public statement about it. After Taylor's death, Fillmore became president and supported the compromise and all other Whig-supported legislation. Despite his loyalty to his party, he was denied the nomination in 1852. He ran unsuccessfully for president in 1856 as the candidate of the American Party, a third party that opposed the immigration of German and Irish Catholics.

Zach's Quick Step," were heard in the streets of towns and cities across America.

Election Day, November 7, was anticipated with great excitement. Congress had passed an act in 1845 that for the first time brought all Americans, except those in Massachusetts, to the polls on the same day. In past presidential elections, it took days or weeks before most Americans knew who the winner was. Thanks to a recent invention, the telegraph, election results reached most people within hours.

Taylor won the **electoral vote** 163 to 127; he carried half of the thirty states—seven in the North and eight in the South. Van Buren won no electoral votes; however, he took enough Democratic votes away from Cass in New York to give Taylor the state's crucial 36 electoral votes. The **popular vote** was far closer, with Taylor getting 1,362,101 votes to Cass's 1,222,674 votes. Van Buren received 291,616 votes.

A political cartoon from 1848 satirizes the three-way race for the presidency showing Martin Van Buren in the lead.

INAUGURATION DAY

President-elect Taylor officially resigned from the army at the end of January 1849. About to become the twelfth president of the United States, Taylor had less political experience than any previous president. He had never previously run for political office, had never shown any interest in politics, and had never voted in a presidential election before his own. In a letter to a friend written during the campaign, Taylor gave some signs of what kind of president he would be: "If elected I would not be the mere president of a party—I would endeavor to act independently of party domination, & and should feel bound to administer the Government untrammeled by party schemes."

Inauguration Day, March 4, fell on a Sunday. Since Sunday was a traditional day of rest and churchgoing, Taylor, who was an Episcopalian, chose to wait till Monday to be inaugurated. Thus the nation was without a leader for twenty-four hours, from the time Polk left office until Taylor took the oath.

PRESIDENT FOR A DAY

The Constitution states that if the president and the vice president are unable to serve, then the office of president passes on to the **president pro tempore** of the Senate. On March 4, 1849, the person who held that post was David Rice Atchison, a senator from Missouri. A few historians believe that Atchison served as president, ever so briefly, and should be noted as such in the history books. If he was president for a day, Atchison's term of office was uneventful. He slept through most of it, having put in a busy week in the Senate. Although his "presidency" is all but forgotten, Atchison's name lives on in two places named in his honor—Atchison County, Missouri, and the city of Atchison, Kansas.

Inaugural Day in Washington was chilly and wet, and a light snow fell on Capitol Hill. After Chief Justice Roger Taney administered the oath of office to Taylor on the east portico of the Capitol, the new president delivered one of the shortest inaugural addresses on record. He gave no hints of his plans in office but did declare his intentions of rising above the interests of sectionalism.

Chosen by the body of the people under the assurance that my Administration would be devoted to the welfare of the whole country, and not to the support of any particular section or merely local interest, I this day renew the declaration I have heretofore made and proclaim my fixed determination to maintain to the extend of my ability the Government in its original purity and to adopt as the basis of my public policy those great republican doctrines which constitute the strength of our national existence.

Taylor went on to say that he looked to Congress "to adopt such measures of conciliation as may harmonize conflicting interests and tend to perpetuate that Union which should be the paramount object of our hopes and affections." Polk, the outgoing president, was not impressed by Taylor's performance. "General Taylor is, I have no doubt, a well-meaning old man," he wrote later that day in his diary. "He is, however, uneducated, exceedingly ignorant of public affairs, and I should judge of very ordinary capacity."

In forming his cabinet, Taylor tried to find a geographic balance. Because of his political inexperience, however, he had to rely on others to find the best man for each job. He chose Senator John M. Clayton of Delaware, another contender for the 1848

Zachary Taylor (center) was helped by others in choosing members of his cabinet.

presidential nomination, as his secretary of state. William M. Meredith, a Philadelphia lawyer, was named secretary of the treasury, and Reverdy Johnson of Maryland became attorney general. The newly created Department of the Interior was headed by Senator Thomas Ewing of Ohio. Daniel Webster and Henry Clay, the two best-known Whig leaders, were missing from the cabinet. Neither man had a high regard for Taylor, and Taylor returned their distrust.

SLAVERY AND THE NEW TERRITORIES

The institution of slavery had been a controversial issue in American society since the signers of the Declaration of Independence debated putting in a section of that document condemning it.

While slavery had previously existed in the North, by the 1840s it had all but disappeared there. The northern states were becoming more industrialized and had less need for a slave-based economy. The South remained largely agricultural, and slave labor helped support its farms and plantations. By the time of Taylor's presidency, the slave debate had become intense. Northerners called **abolitionists** were condemning slavery as morally wrong and actively campaigned to abolish it.

The number of so-called slave and free states was equal when Taylor became president; there were fifteen slave states, including the most recent admission, Texas, and fifteen free states. The Treaty of Guadalupe brought in three new territories that threatened to upset that balance—California, Utah, and New Mexico. California, with its growing population, wanted to be admitted as a state, not a territory, and had enough residents to qualify for statehood. Mexico had abolished slavery there some years earlier, and most Californians, whether they came from slave states or free ones, wanted to live in a free state without slavery. Southern legislators in the Congress were opposed to California becoming a free state since it would upset the balance of power they shared with the free states and possibly threaten the future of slavery in their own states.

Although a Southerner by birth and upbringing, President Taylor was a Northerner by temperament. He believed strongly in the Union above all sectional concerns. In late 1849, he came out in favor of both California and New Mexico, which had a sparse population, becoming free states. Southern leaders feared they would become a minority in Congress. Other legislators,

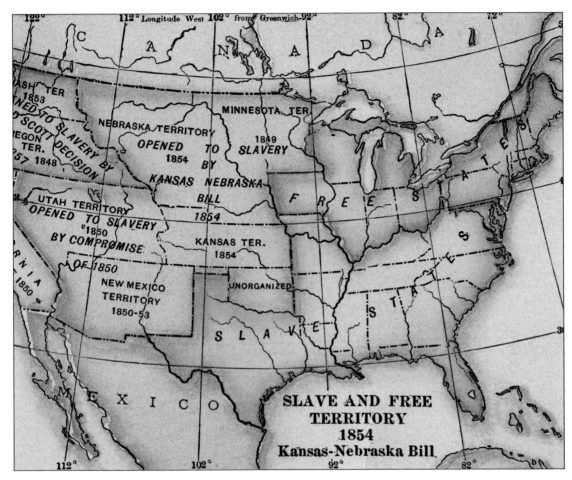

The following labels appear on the map:

122° 112° Longitude West 102° from Greenwich 92° 82° 72°

CANADA

C

WASH TER
1853
OWNED TO SLAVERY BY
SCOTT DECISION
OREGON
TER.
1857 1848

NEBRASKA TERRITORY
OPENED TO
1854
KANSAS NEBRASKA
BILL
1854

MINNESOTA TER

1849
SLAVERY

UTAH TERRITORY
OPENED TO SLAVERY
1850
BY COMPROMISE
OF 1850

KANSAS TER.
1854

FREE STATES

NEW MEXICO
TERRITORY
1850-53

UNORGANIZED

CALIFORNIA
1850

SLAVE STATES

MEXICO

SLAVE AND FREE
TERRITORY
1854
Kansas-Nebraska Bill

112° 102° 92° 82°

A map illustrates slave and free states as of 1854.

including some in the North, felt Taylor's position was not in keeping with what they saw as the caretaker role of president and that he should leave the matter to Congress to decide. While many northern Whigs in Congress supported the president's plan, the majority of lawmakers chose to ignore it, and the debate over the issue of slavery in the territories continued to cause unrest.

The California Gold Rush

The great explosion of population in California was due to one central event—the California gold rush. Flakes of gold were first discovered at Sutter's Mill, located on the southern fork of the American River near San Francisco, on January 24, 1848, by James Marshall, a carpenter who worked for John Sutter. Sutter tried to keep the discovery a secret, but the news soon leaked out. By July, four thousand men were digging for gold in the region. The thousands more who arrived overland or by boat in 1849 were given the name forty-niners. Few of the men who panned for gold found enough to make them rich. Nevertheless, many of the newcomers, finding California's fertile soil and warm, sunny climate to their liking, stayed on after leaving the goldfields and went into farming and other businesses. The population of the territory before the gold rush started was less than 15,000. By the end of 1849, it had surged to more than 100,000. California was on its way to becoming one of the richest and most populous states in the nation.

A Presidential Tour

On August 9, 1849, President Taylor, with a small party that included his son-in-law Dr. Robert Wood, left by train for a kind of early fact-finding tour of the northern states. Taylor wanted to learn about the attitudes of Northerners and also wanted an excuse to escape the humid heat of Washington, which was threatened by a **cholera** invasion.

The presidential party traveled north through Maryland, Pennsylvania, and New York. Everywhere Taylor went, he was celebrated by galas and parties. The heat of summer and the excitement of the crowds wore down the sixty-four-year-old president. While staying in Harrisburg, Pennsylvania, Taylor came down with a serious case of diarrhea and vomiting. Dr. Wood medicated him, and he recovered but soon after cut his tour short and returned to Washington.

Taylor's northern tour showed that although he had come to the presidency with little experience, Taylor was eager to learn and was growing in the job. However, although his mind and will were strong, his physical health was deteriorating.

As president of the United States, Zachary Taylor firmly believed in the preservation of the Union, a point he made in his only State of the Union Address.

Engraved by T.W. Hunt

from a Dag by Brady

Okee-cho-hee   Dec. 25th 1837.

Affairs at Home and Abroad

On December 4, 1849, President Taylor delivered his first and only State of the Union message to Congress. In it, he called for raising the tariff to offset debts incurred by the expenses of the Mexican War, as well as the establishment of an agricultural bureau within the Department of the Interior and the development of a transcontinental railroad to link the nation. He ended his address with a stirring declaration that the Union must be preserved at all costs.

For more than half a century, during which kingdoms and empires have fallen, this Union has stood unshaken. The patriots who formed it have long since descended to the grave; yet still it remains, the proudest monument to their memory and the object of affection and admiration with everyone worthy to bear the American name. In my judgment its dissolution would be the greatest of calamities, and to avert that should be the study of every American. Upon its preservation must depend our own happiness and that of countless generations to come. Whatever dangers may threaten it, I shall stand by it and maintain it in its integrity to the full extent of the obligations imposed and the powers conferred upon me by the Constitution.

That unity was threatened in New Mexico when Texans laid claim to some of its territory. In September 1849 New Mexicans drew up a second petition to be administered as a free, not a slave, territory. Taylor gave his support to the New Mexicans and went a step further and urged that their territory be admitted to the Union as a state. Texan legislators, upset by the idea of a free state of New Mexico, threatened to secede from the United States. Taylor was not fazed by their threat and said he would send federal troops to Texas to prevent an insurrection.

Two members of Congress from Georgia, Representative Alexander Hamilton Stephens and Senator Robert Toombs, met with Taylor to discuss the matter. "Southern officers will refuse to obey your orders if you send troops to coerce Texas," Stephens told the president. "Then I will command the army in person," Taylor replied, "and any man who is taken in treason against the Union I will hang. . . ."

In the end, there was no armed conflict between federal troops and Southerners, but the tensions over the slave question continued. Henry Clay presented several compromises in the Senate to bring the two sides together, including one that called for California to enter the Union as a free state and the territories of New Mexico and Utah to be admitted under popular sovereignty. His compromise bill failed to pass in the Senate in early 1850. As Taylor's continued opposition to slavery in the new territories was a factor in that failure, the animosity between Clay and Taylor continued to grow.

Indian Affairs

President Taylor was cautious when dealing with Native Americans. In July 1849, rumors about another Seminole uprising in Florida caused residents to insist Taylor send more troops and call

In 1850 Henry Clay urged the U.S. Senate to adopt his compromise as a way to avoid a civil war.

New Mexico

The first Spanish settlement in what is now New Mexico was established in 1598. For more than two centuries it remained a remote outpost of Spanish America, whose few colonists struggled with the harsh, mountainous terrain and raids by hostile Apache and Navajo Indians. When Mexico became independent from Spain in 1821, it encouraged Americans to enter and trade in the New Mexico region. The Santa Fe Trail brought settlers to the West. It also brought manufactured goods to the people of New Mexico. The colonial capital, Santa Fe, surrendered without bloodshed to the U.S. Army during the Mexican War. In 1850 the U.S. Congress created the New Mexico Territory. Twelve years later the territory of Arizona was carved out of New Mexico's western half. New Mexico continued to be a wild and dangerous place where Geronimo and other renegade Apaches and outlaws, such as Billy the Kid, roamed. It was one of the last territories in the continental United States to achieve statehood, on January 6, 1912.

out the state militia. Taylor agreed to send some troops to stabilize the situation but ruled out militia involvement. Only a few renegade Indians had gone on a rampage as it turned out.

The following month, a Texan wrote Taylor that Indians had massacred more than two hundred people in his state. The number killed proved far fewer, and while the president gave orders for the Texas Rangers to be enlisted, there was little further trouble with the Indians.

Trouble with France and Great Britain

Taylor proved he was an outspoken and fearless leader in foreign affairs as well as domestic ones. His dissatisfaction with France's U.S. representative, William Tell Poussin, came to a head over a minor issue. The U.S.S. *Iris*, a naval ship, rescued the French ship *Eugenie* from a reef near Vera Cruz, Mexico. The *Iris*'s commander, Edward William Carpender, held the vessel for a claim of **salvage**. When the claim was rejected by local officials, Carpender released the ship. Poussin insisted that Carpender be severely reprimanded for his actions. Taylor and Secretary of State Clayton refused and asked that Poussin be recalled. The French government granted the request but refused to receive the new U.S. representative to France, William Cabell Rives, until Taylor apologized for his rude treatment of Poussin. Taylor flatly refused, and for a brief time it looked as though the incident might lead to war between France and the United States. In the end, Louis-Napoléon Bonaparte, the president of the French Republic, agreed to receive Rives in November 1849, and a crisis was averted.

While relations with France were somewhat strained, the United States appeared to be getting along well with its former enemy Great Britain. Since the War of 1812, the two countries had found mutual benefits in peaceful trade and diplomacy. In 1849 events occurred that threatened that peace.

Great Britain had controlled Canada since it defeated France in the French and Indian War, which ended in 1763. Some Canadians, both of English and of French extraction, were unhappy with the British, who controlled their economy and politics.

In October 1849, more than one thousand Canadians signed an "annexation manifesto" that called for "a friendly and peaceful separation" from Great Britain and annexation by the United States. Great Britain was alarmed that these separatists were supported by a number of Americans. Taylor quickly assured the British that the United States would remain neutral in the matter and any Americans who abetted a Canadian revolt would be stopped by U.S. troops. The British **chargé d'affaires**, John F. Crampton, praised Taylor "for the fearless and determined manner in which he follows up a course when he has . . . made up his mind that it is his duty to pursue it. . . ."

The Clayton-Bulwer Treaty

Another issue of contention arose between the United States and Great Britain. The California gold rush brought to the fore a long-held dream of Americans—a canal across the isthmus of Central America. The forty-niners had two routes to get to California: either overland, a dangerous prospect in the 1840s, or by boat around South America and up the Pacific coast, a long and tortuous journey. A canal across Central America would shorten the voyage by weeks.

The country of Nicaragua was chosen as the best site for the canal, and the United States entered into negotiations with the Nicaraguan government. Great Britain was also interested in such a canal for trade and commerce and in January 1848 seized the Nicaraguan town of San Juan del Norte and claimed it as part of a nearby British colony known as the Mosquito Coast Territory. Not wanting to alienate the British, Taylor's administration began negotiations with the two countries, but poor communications caused the talks to flounder.

The First U.S. Postage Stamps

In 1849 President Taylor asked Congress to reduce the postal rate to five cents for any letter mailed in the United States. This action affected the price of a new addition to American  life—postage stamps, the first of which were issued only a little more than a year earlier. The first nation to issue postage stamps was Great Britain, in 1840. Senator Daniel Webster introduced a resolution to Congress the same year to investigate adopting postage stamps for American mail. The postmaster general, hearing how stamps had improved the postal system in Great Britain, urged Congress to act, but lawmakers debated the issue for seven years. Before stamps, mailing a one-page letter was expensive. The postal rate, depending on how far the letter was going, could be as high as twenty-five cents, a lot of money in those days. Most Americans could not afford to send mail. In 1845 Congress set two postal rates for distance—five cents and ten cents. The first two stamps in these denominations were issued two years later. The five-cent stamp bore the portrait of Benjamin Franklin, the first postmaster general. The ten-cent stamp bore the portrait of George Washington. By 1855 postage stamps were required on all letters mailed in the United States.

In January 1850, a British **envoy** named Henry L. Bulwer arrived to meet with Secretary of State Clayton. The two men drafted a treaty, which Taylor found vague and sent back for revision. The final draft was sent to Congress on July 5, 1850. The treaty called for Britain and the United States to work together to develop the canal and forbade other colonial designs on "any part of Central America." The Clayton-Bulwer Treaty was the major achievement in foreign affairs of Taylor's presidency. The Nicaragua canal was never built, however. Fifty years later the United States completed the Panama Canal across neighboring Panama.

THE LÓPEZ AFFAIR

Another American foray into Latin America involved an attempted takeover of the Spanish colony of Cuba. Narciso López, a former Spanish officer and landowner, was involved in revolutionary activities against the Spanish and was forced to flee Cuba. In the United States, López plotted an invasion of the island to incite the Cubans to rebel against the Spanish and drive them out. Southern leaders, seeing Cuba as a future slave state that would counterbalance the admittance of California as a free state, supported López's plot. López enlisted six hundred men in his cause and was ready to invade Cuba in the summer of 1849 when President Taylor stepped in to halt his illegal activities.

In early 1850 López took three ships to Cuba and tried again. Some of his men were captured by the Spanish; López and the rest fled back to the United States. There López was arrested and put on trial for violating the Neutrality Law, whereby Americans were forbidden to get involved in the affairs of other countries, including Spain and its colonies. He was acquitted by a sympathetic southern jury. Meanwhile, Taylor urged Spain to release the fifty captives of López's plot, whom the government was planning to execute for piracy. Taylor insisted they had committed no crimes despite their intent to do so. The Spanish heeded his warning and released the prisoners. López was not so lucky. On his third attempt to invade Cuba, in 1851, he was captured and executed.

Social Life in the White House

The Taylor White House was a busy one, filled with immediate family and numerous relatives, including his daughter Betty and her husband, William Bliss who was Taylor's private secretary, and the president's younger brother Joseph and his family. Joseph served as a presidential aide while Congress was in session. There were also four grandchildren who came for lengthy visits from Baltimore, where they lived with Taylor's daughter Ann Taylor Wood and her husband, Robert. Ann's eldest son, John Wood, served in the Mexican War, while Bob, the second son, who was Taylor's favorite, went to West Point on his grandfather's recommendation.

Taylor continued to show little interest in clothes when he became president. He would frequently be seen wandering among the common people on the White House lawn wearing an oversize black broadcloth suit that he said was comfortable because of its looseness. A tall silk hat worn pushed back on his head gave him a rakish look.

"He really is a most simple-minded old man," Horace Mann, a Massachusetts congressman, wrote to a friend after dining with the president. "He has the least show or pretension about him of any man I ever saw; talks as artlessly as a child about affairs of

State, and does not seem to pretend to a knowledge of any thing of which he is ignorant. He is a remarkable man in some respects; and it is remarkable that such a man should be President of the United States."

The first lady, Margaret Taylor, was even less pretentious than her husband. A semi-invalid, she installed herself on the second floor of the White House, where she spent a good deal of her time knitting and tending to her family. She rarely left her room but did receive guests there, including Jefferson Davis's second wife, Varina Howell Davis. Davis called the first lady's room "bright and pretty" and described her as "full of interest in the passing show in which she had not the strength to take part, [and said that she] talked most agreeably and kindly to the many friends admitted to her presence." Margaret left the duties of White House hostess to her daughter Mary.

A Scandal

In April 1850, a scandal erupted in the Taylor White House. It concerned the long-deceased George Galphin, a Georgia land-owner who submitted a claim to the British Crown for land lost to local Indians before the Revolutionary War. Because Galphin had sided with the colonists in the Revolution, the British never repaid his claim. Later the state of Georgia and then the U.S. government assumed the claim but deferred payment for many years. A Georgia lawyer named George Crawford represented Galphin's descendants in the case for fifteen years. The claim was finally paid but not the interest on it, which by 1850 had reached a whopping $191,352.89. That year the claim was paid by the secretary of the treasury, with half of the money going to Crawford as the legal agent. The payment to Crawford raised eyebrows in Washington

MARY ELIZABETH BLISS, FIRST DAUGHTER

Mary Bliss, or Betty, as she was called by her family, filled the role of White House hostess with, in the words of one admirer, "the artlessness of a rustic belle and the grace of a duchess." The youngest Taylor girl, Mary was born in 1824 and was educated at a finishing school in Philadelphia. She married Lieutenant Colonel William Wallace Smith Bliss in December 1848, a month after her father was elected president. At his inaugural ball Mary wore a white dress and a white rose in her hair and thereafter was called "Wild Rose of the White House."

William Bliss, as indispensable to his father-in-law as Mary was to her mother, died of yellow fever while crossing Panama three years after Taylor's death. Mary later married Philip Pendleton Dandridge, a Virginian, and was a southern sympathizer during the Civil War. Mary died in 1909 at age eighty-five, childless.

because Crawford was now Taylor's secretary of war. All that money changing hands between two cabinet members was viewed as questionable ethics, and Taylor himself became embroiled in the scandal. As the Fourth of July holiday approached, Congress was preparing to meet to debate whether it should censure the president for his involvement in the Galphin affair.

GEN. GEO. WASHINGTON

President Zachary Taylor attended the laying of the cornerstone of the Washington Monument. He soon fell ill and died thereafter.

LAYING CORNER STONE, WASHINGTON MONUMENT

An Untimely End

$\mathcal{J}$uly 4, 1850, was a hot and humid day in Washington. President Taylor had slept poorly the night before, possibly worrying about the Galphin scandal and whether he would have to replace Secretary of War Crawford and other members of his cabinet. It was no ordinary Independence Day in the capital. The placing of the **cornerstone** of the Washington Monument was to take place amid much ceremony and pomp.

The sixty-five-year-old Taylor presided over the event and looked on as the workmen laid the cornerstone. Standing bareheaded in the broiling sun, the president listened patiently to two hours of patriotic speeches and military band music. After the ceremony, he took one of his customary walks around the city and returned to the White House, hot, tired, and hungry. He devoured green apples, cold cherries, and quarts of iced milk. By evening, Taylor was experiencing severe stomach cramps. He had suffered similar symptoms on his presidential tour the previous September, and his doctors were not unduly concerned. By Saturday, July 6, Taylor felt well enough to leave his sickbed and sign the Clayton-Bulwer Treaty, which had been passed by Congress. It was his last act as president.

By Sunday, his condition worsened. By Tuesday, July 9, it was clear the president was dying. The end came at 10:35 p.m., with family and friends at his bedside. Taylor's last recorded words were, "I am about to die—I expect the summons soon. I have endeavored to discharge all my official duties faithfully.

I regret nothing, but am sorry that I am about to leave my friends." Taylor had served as president for only sixteen months. To date, his presidency is one of the shortest in history. Only those of James A. Garfield (six months) and William Henry Harrison (one month) were shorter.

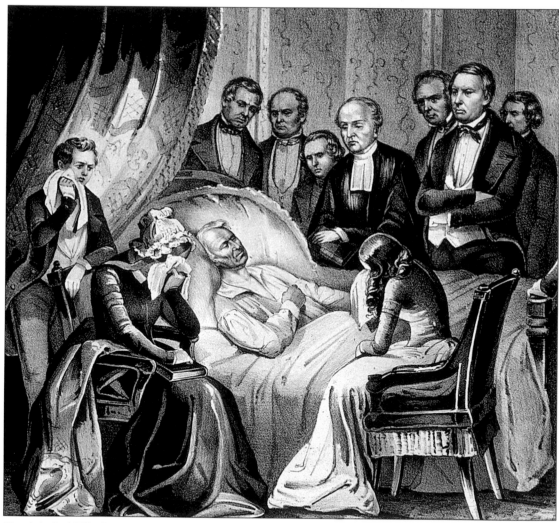

On July 9, 1850, President Zachary Taylor died at his home surrounded by his wife, son, colleagues, and friends.

The Taylor "Murder" Mystery

The cause of Taylor's death has remained something of a mystery. Some historians distrust the official cause of death, gastroenteritis, and have suggested he may have died of cholera morbus, typhus, or a stomach infection. Some even believe his death was brought about by the mercury, opium, and quinine that his doctors dosed him with to try to save him. In January 1991, nearly a century and a half after his death, Clara Rising, researching a biography of Taylor, announced to the world that he might have been murdered. Her research indicated that someone could have sprinkled arsenic on the cherries or another dish he ate that fateful July 4th. Rising believed the motive for the murder was Taylor's position that slavery should be kept out of California and New Mexico and his blocking of the passing of a congressional compromise with the slave states. The list of suspects included Senator Henry Clay, who created the compromise bill, and Vice President Millard Fillmore, who had the most to gain from Taylor's death.

Rising and Taylor's heirs persuaded a Kentucky county coroner to have his corpse exhumed, and the coroner tested his tissue and bones for an undue amount of arsenic. The test proved negative, and Taylor's remains were again laid to rest. Rising's book, *The Taylor File: The Mysterious Death of a President*, in which she explains her research and reasoning, was published in 2007.

A President's Funeral

Margaret Taylor was devastated by her husband's death and refused to have his remains **embalmed**. Three times she asked for his coffin to be opened so that she could gaze on him. The rest of the family was just as stunned. "We had thought of our mother's dying," said Mary Bliss later, "for she is . . . seldom well, but our father . . . we never expected him to die!"

Taylor's funeral was a somber spectacle, befitting a military hero and president. One hundred carriages followed the **catafalque** drawn by eight white horses that bore Taylor's body. As many as 100,000 people lined the streets of the funeral procession. Taylor's brother, his son-in-law William Bliss, and his grandsons were the only family members to attend the ceremony. Margaret remained in her room upstairs in the White House, too weak and upset to attend. That evening she and the Blisses moved out of the White House and into the home of a cabinet member. Five days later she left Washington, never to return.

Taylor's grand funeral pageant took place in Washington, D.C., on July 23, 1850.

Richard Taylor, the Forgotten First Son

Among those family members missing at Taylor's funeral was his son, Richard. Given the distant relationship of father and son, his absence comes as no surprise. A warm and compassionate man who doted on his grandchildren, Taylor inexplicably showed little affection toward his only son. When the boy was ten, his father sent him away to a private school in Louisville, and they saw each other only once in the next eleven years. Later Taylor wrote, "Better to make no very  great calculations as regards the prominent positions our children are to occupy . . . they are but rarely realized." When he became president, Taylor saw that his son remained on the family's southern plantation overseeing its operation. Richard was not invited to his father's inaugural and made only one appearance at the White House, to report on a flood that had swept through the plantation. He never saw his father again. Taylor had not wanted his son to be a professional soldier, but Richard acquitted himself well as a lieutenant general in the Civil War. He served on the side of the Confederacy, something that would have surely dismayed his father.

Millard Fillmore was sworn in the day after Taylor's death as the thirteenth president. Taylor was buried temporarily in the Congressional Burial Ground. Shortly after, his remains were reburied on his plantation near Louisville.

Among the many tributes delivered to the late president was one by Horace Greeley, who often criticized Taylor in the pages of his newspaper, the New York *Tribune*. "A Southern man and a slaveholder," Greeley wrote, "his mind was above the narrow prejudices of district and class and steadily aimed at the good of the nation as a whole."

LEGACY

Zachary Taylor was the first career military man to occupy the White House. While George Washington, Andrew Jackson, and William Henry Harrison were also war heroes, their military service made up only a part of their resumes before reaching the presidency. He has been called a courageous leader and a strong Unionist. He was also blunt, stubborn, and at times a poor diplomat. His time in office was short, and so it is impossible to speculate on what he might have accomplished had he lived to complete his term. The effect on the course of history of his strong Unionist stance and his blunt opposition to secession is unknown. He certainly would have vetoed the Compromise of 1850. Whether such an action would have hastened the Civil War or resulted in a peaceful solution is an unanswerable question. What is certain is that the three presidents who followed Taylor—Fillmore, Franklin Pierce, and James Buchanan—were unable to reconcile northern and southern interests and succeeded only in postponing sectional conflict.

The Compromise of 1850

On January 29, 1850, Henry Clay introduced in Congress a series of compromises to make peace between slavery and antislavery interests. It took months of debate in both houses and the death of President Taylor, who opposed any compromise with the pro-slave South, to finally make the Compromise of 1850 law. According to its provisions California would enter the Union as a free state, while the territories of New Mexico and Utah would determine their status on slavery by the popular vote of residents. Texas would renounce all claims to New Mexico in return for debt relief. The slave trade, but not slavery itself, would be abolished in the District of Columbia. Finally, the Fugitive Slave Act was passed; it required citizens to cooperate with the return of runaway slaves under federal law.

Historians are divided on the legacy of the Compromise of 1850. Some say it delayed the Civil War for a decade. Others say its attempt to appease both sides on the slavery issue ultimately failed and only made war between the North and the South inevitable.

As president, Taylor displayed a strength and courage that is admirable. He came into the office a complete novice but showed signs of growth and maturity over time. He displayed a restraint and maturity in his handling of the López affair and the negotiations that led to the Clayton-Bulwer Treaty with Great Britain, the major achievement of his presidency. He correctly anticipated California's entrance to the Union shortly after his death as a free state. Texas dropped its claim to the New Mexico Territory, although decades passed before New Mexico, neighboring Arizona, and Utah achieved statehood.

If Taylor's achievements as president were few, his achievements as a soldier remain impressive. He was a far more successful field commander than the other Whig president, William Henry Harrison. If some of his victories, especially against Native Americans, are exaggerated and if luck played as great a part in some of his wins as strategy and skill, Taylor still earned his fame as a national hero in the Mexican War. His courage and daring in his upset of Santa Anna at the Battle of Buena Vista showed him to be a leader capable of inspiring his soldiers to great deeds.

In his **eulogy** for Taylor, Abraham Lincoln summed up the soldier-president with these words:

> The fruits of his labor, his name, his memory and example, are all that is left us—his example, verifying the great truth that "he that humbleth himself, shall be exalted" teaching that to serve one's country with a singleness of purpose gives assurances of that country's gratitude, secures its best honors, and makes "a dying bed, soft as downy pillows are."

President Zachary Taylor came into office with no political experience, only that from the battlefield. However, he exhibited great leadership and courage while trying to hold the Union together at all costs.

1784

Zachary Taylor is born in Orange County, Virginia (November 24)

1808

Is commissioned a first lieutenant in the U.S. Army

1810

Marries Margaret Smith (June 21)

1815

Is promoted to brevet major during the War of 1812

1819

Is promoted to lieutenant colonel

1832

Is promoted to colonel; earns praise for his service in the Black Hawk War

1784

1846

Is victorious at Resaca de la Palma and Monterrey during the Mexican War

1847

Defeats General Santa Anna at the Battle of Buena Vista on February 22 and 23

1848

Is elected the twelfth president of the United States

1850

Dies of natural causes in the White House (July 9)

1850

Notes

CHAPTER ONE

p. 11, "our little army . . .": John S. D. Eisenhower, *Zachary Taylor* (New York: Holt, 2008), p. 6.

p. 11, "perhaps unnecessary evil . . .": Eisenhower, *Zachary Taylor*, p. 6.

p. 13, "My wife was as much a soldier . . .": Carl Sferrazza Anthony, *America's First Families* (New York: Touchstone, 2000), p. 84.

CHAPTER TWO

p. 15, "Nothing saved the fort but . . .": Eisenhower, *Zachary Taylor*, p. 10.

p. 17, "I have commenced making corn . . .": Eisenhower, *Zachary Taylor*, p. 17.

p. 20, "burn and destroy the establishments . . .": Elbert B. Smith, *The Presidencies of Zachary Taylor and Millard Fillmore* (Lawrence, KS: University of Kansas Press, 1988), p. 29.

p. 25, "one of the . . . costliest and most frustrating . . .": Eisenhower, *Zachary Taylor*, p. 25.

p. 26, "old codger": John and Alice Durant, *Pictorial History of American Presidents* (New York: A. S. Barnes, 1955), p. 89.

p. 26, "Never judge a stranger . . .": Durant, *Pictorial History of American Presidents*, p. 89.

p. 26, "We must abandon general operations . . .": Robert M. Utley and Wilcomb E. Washburn, *The American Heritage History of the Indian Wars* (New York: American Heritage, 1977), p. 146.

p. 27, "miserable country . . . where an officer . . .": Smith, *The Presidencies of Zachary Taylor and Millard Fillmore*, p. 32.

CHAPTER THREE

p. 35, "I was within ten feet . . .": Silas Bent McKinley, *Old Rough and Ready: The Life and Times of Zachary Taylor* (New York: Vanguard Press, 1946), p. 167.

p. 36, ". . . my dear General . . .": Eisenhower, *Zachary Taylor*, pp. 63–64.

p. 38, "with the consideration . . .": Eisenhower, *Zachary Taylor*, p. 69.

p. 38, "In reply to your note . . .": Eisenhower, *Zachary Taylor*, p. 69.

p. 38, "A little more grape[shot] . . .": McKinley, *Old Rough and Ready*, p. 187.

p. 38, "General, we are whipped . . .": McKinley, *Old Rough and Ready*, p. 187.

p. 39, "to the consciousness of . . .": Smith, *The Presidencies of Zachary Taylor and Millard Fillmore*, p. 38.

Chapter Four

p. 42, "it must be by the . . .": Smith, *The Presidencies of Zachary Taylor and Millard Fillmore*, p. 39.

p. 44, "If you desire a bank . . .": Paul F. Boller, Jr., *Presidential Campaigns* (New York: Oxford University Press, 1984), p. 85.

p. 44, "If General Cass went . . .": Boller, *Presidential Campaigns*, p. 87.

p. 49, "military autocrat": Boller, *Presidential Campaigns*, p. 85.

p. 49, "a sly, artful, intriguing politician": Boller, *Presidential Campaigns*, p. 86.

p. 50, "If elected I would not be . . .": Eisenhower, *Zachary Taylor*, p. 81.

p. 52, "Chosen by the body of the people . . .": Taylor's inaugural address, http://www.bartleby.com/124/pres28.html (accessed January 16, 2009).

p. 52, "to adopt such measures . . .": Smith, *The Presidencies of Zachary Taylor and Millard Fillmore*, p. 51.

p. 52, "General Taylor is, I have no doubt . . .": Eisenhower, *Zachary Taylor*, p. 94.

Chapter Five

p. 59, "For more than half a century . . .": David C. Whitney and Robin Vaughn Whitney, *The American Presidents* (Pleasantville, NY: Reader's Digest, 1996), p. 104.

p. 60, "Southern officers will refuse . . .": McKinley, *Old Rough and Ready*, p. 283.

p. 64, "a friendly and peaceful separation": Smith, *The Presidencies of Zachary Taylor and Millard Fillmore*, p. 74.

p. 64, "for the fearless and determined manner . . .": Smith, *The Presidencies of Zachary Taylor and Millard Fillmore*, p. 75.

p. 66, "any part of Central America.": Eisenhower, *Zachary Taylor*, p. 120.

p. 67, "He really is a most simple-minded old man . . .": McKinley, *Old Rough and Ready*, p. 271.

p. 68, "the artlessness of a rustic belle . . .": Paul F. Boller Jr., *Presidential Wives: An Anecdotal History* (New York: Oxford University Press, 1988), p. 97.

p. 68, "Wild Rose of the White House": Lu Ann Paletta, *The World Almanac of First Ladies* (New York: Pharos Books, 1990), p. 189.

p. 69, "bright and pretty . . . full of interest . . .": Boller, *Presidential Wives*, p. 97.

Chapter Six

p. 71, "I am about to die . . .": Smith, *The Presidencies of Zachary Taylor and Millard Fillmore*, p. 157.

p. 74, "We had thought of our mother's dying . . .": Boller, *Presidential Wives*, p. 97.

p. 75, "Better to make no very great . . .": Anthony, *America's First Families*, p. 95.

p. 76, "A Southern man and a slaveholder . . .": Smith, *The Presidencies of Zachary Taylor and Millard Fillmore*, p. 158.

p. 78, "The fruits of his labor, his name . . .": McKinley, *Old Rough and Ready*, p. 298.

GLOSSARY

abolitionists people who worked, whether peacefully or violently, to end slavery in the United States before the Civil War

aide-de-camp a military assistant; typically a junior officer serving as an aide to a high-ranking officer

annex to incorporate territory into a city, state, or country

armistice a truce ending hostilities between warring enemies

autocrat an absolute ruler; a dictator

ballot a vote, of citizens in an election or of delegates at a political convention

blockhouse fortlike building with an upper story that has openings to allow its defenders to use small arms

brevet a generally temporary military rank higher than the rank for which its holder receives pay

catafalque a raised structure on which a dead body lies or is carried

censure an official statement of disapproval by Congress of one of its members or of the president

chargé d'affaires an important diplomatic official of lower rank than an ambassador

cholera a frequently contagious disease of the digestive tract caused by a bacterium found in contaminated drinking water, once widespread in the United States

coerce to force, compel, or intimidate someone to act in a certain way

comptroller a government official who supervises financial matters

cornerstone a foundation stone, one marking the onset of construction of a monument or great building

Democrat a member of the Democratic Party, a major U.S. political party founded in 1828

electoral college in the United States, the officials, or electors, within each state whose votes elect the president and vice president

electoral vote in U.S. presidential elections, the votes cast in each state by the officials who form the electoral college. Strictly speaking, the electoral vote, not the popular vote (the votes cast by citizens), decides a presidential election

embalm to treat a dead body with chemicals or other substances to slow its decay

envoy a diplomat; particularly, one charged with a special mission

eulogy a speech made in tribute to someone who has died

hacienda a large landed estate in Spanish America

impressment a form of military recruitment. In the period prior to the War of 1812, the British frequently abducted sailors from American merchant ships to serve in the Royal Navy

malaria a parasitic disease transmitted to humans by the bite of a mosquito and characterized by attacks of chills and fever

man-of-war a warship

Mexican War a conflict (1846–1848) involving the United States and Mexico

militia a body of nonprofessional citizen-soldiers

popular sovereignty a pre–Civil War policy whereby the residents of a territory determined for themselves by vote whether or not to allow slavery there

popular vote in U.S. presidential elections, the total number of votes cast by citizens, as opposed to those cast by electors

president pro tempore the senator chosen by his or her senatorial colleagues to preside over the Senate when the vice president is absent

salvage compensation for the goods saved from a sinking ship paid to the captain or others who save them

tariff a duty imposed primarily on imported goods

Treaty of Guadalupe Hidalgo the treaty that ended the Mexican War. Under its terms Mexico ceded to the United States territory that constitutes the present-day American Southwest, including all or part of New Mexico, Arizona, Nevada, California, and Utah

War of 1812 a conflict between the United States and Great Britain; it lasted from 1812 to 1815

Whig a major American political party, formed in opposition to Andrew Jackson and the Democratic Party, that existed from about 1834 to 1855

FURTHER INFORMATION

BOOKS

Brunelli, Carol. *Zachary Taylor: Our Twelfth President*. Mankato, MN: Child's World, 2008.

Elston, Heidi. *Zachary Taylor*. Edina, MN: Abdo, 2009.

Gottfried, Ted. *Millard Fillmore*. New York: Marshall Cavendish Benchmark, 2008.

DVD

The American President. PBS Home Video, 2000.

WEBSITES

American President: An Online Reference Resource

www.millercenter.virginia.edu/academic/americanpresident/cleveland

This site, maintained by the University of Virginia, includes concise biographies of Taylor, his wife, his vice president, and all the members of his cabinet.

American Presidents

www.americanpresidents.org/presidents/president.
   asp?PresidentNumber=12

This statistical profile includes a detailed bibliography and a list of historic
   sites associated with Taylor.

Museum of History—Hall of U.S. Presidents

http://zacharytaylor.org/

This site features a portrait of Taylor, a detailed biography, and a
   message in which he nominates members of his cabinet.

The White House

www.whitehouse.gov/about/presidents/ZacharyTaylor/

The White House website provides biographical and historical
   information on all the American presidents.

BIBLIOGRAPHY

Angelo, Bonnie. *First Families: The Importance of the White House on Their Lives*. New York: Morrow, 2005.

Anthony, Carl Sferrazza. *America's First Families*. New York: Touchstone Books, 2000.

Boller, Paul F., Jr. *Presidential Campaigns*. New York: Oxford University Press, 1984.

———. *Presidential Wives: An Anecdotal History*. New York: Oxford University Press, 1988.

Durant, John, and Alice Durant. *Pictorial History of American Presidents*. New York: A. S. Barnes, 1955.

Dwyer, Jim, ed. *Strange Stories: Amazing Facts of America's Past*. Pleasantville, NY: Reader's Digest, 1989.

Eisenhower, John S. D. *Zachary Taylor*. New York: Holt, 2008.

Frank, Sid, and Arden Davis Melick. *The Presidents: Tidbits and Trivia*. Maplewood, NJ: Hammond, 1980.

McKinley, Silas Bent. *Old Rough and Ready: The Life and Times of Zachary Taylor*. New York: Vanguard Press, 1946.

Paletta, Lee Ann. *The World Almanac of First Ladies*. New York: Pharos Books, 1990.

Paletta, Lee Ann, and Fred Worth. *The World Almanac Book of Presidential Facts*. New York: Pharos Books, 1988.

Smith, Elbert B. *The Presidencies of Zachary Taylor and Millard Fillmore*. Lawrence, KS: University of Kansas Press, 1988.

Utley, Robert M., and Wilcomb E. Washburn. *The American Heritage History of the Indian Wars*. New York: American Heritage, 1977.

Whitney, David C., and Robin Vaughn Whitney. *The American Presidents*. Pleasantville, NY: Reader's Digest, 1996.

INDEX

Pages in **boldface** are illustrations.

ABOUT THE AUTHOR

Steven Otfinoski is the author of more than 140 children's titles. He previously wrote *Calvin Coolidge, Chester Arthur,* and *Grover Cleveland* for the Marshall Cavendish series Presidents and Their Times. Otfinoski lives in Connecticut with his wife, Beverly, an editor and English teacher.

★ ★ ★ ★ ★ ★ ★ ★ ★ ★ ★ ★ ★ ★ ★ ★ ★ ★ ★